Ursula Schwitalla, Christiane Fath (eds.)

divia award 2023

Diversity in Architecture e.V.

HATJE
CANTZ

Acknowledgments

When we founded the nonprofit organization (NPO) Diversity in Architecture (DIVIA) in Berlin in June 2021, it was our ambitious desire to present the first *divia award* in May 2023. With the ultimate goal to foster much-needed diversity in the field, including giving a voice to other underrepresented groups, our first step is to make women in architecture more visible and give their work the recognition it deserves. A biennial award for women in architecture, which did not exist in Germany until now, should help achieve that goal.

With the enthusiastic commitment of our founding members—next to the two initiators Ursula Schwitalla (Tuebingen) and Christiane Fath (Berlin)—Dirk Boll (London), Sol Camacho (São Paulo), Odile Decq (Paris), Angelika Fitz (Vienna), Anna Heringer (Laufen), and Marc Kimmich (Berlin), and with the support of our donors DIVIA soon became an active platform. In the following year, it was already able to successfully announce a diverse and exciting list of twenty-seven nominees, chosen by an international advisory board. The list was then handed to the jury, who carefully selected the five finalists and, eventually, the winner.

We congratulate all nominees, the four finalists and the winner for being the faces of the first *divia award*. Divia is dedicated to showcasing not only the winner but also the other finalists, which is unique in architecture prizes. In addition to the monetary prize of 20,000 euros given to the winner, a catalogue and a traveling exhibition featuring the work of all five women architects are presented with each award cycle.

The ability to celebrate the debut of the *divia award* as early as 2023 is in large part due to the enthusiastic response of our members in the NPO, the generous support of our donors, and the wonderful DIVIA team. We would also like to express our gratitude to the advisory board and the international jury, who contributed to the process with their expertise and great commitment until the very end on a pro bono basis. Thank you to Hatje Cantz Verlag for its support in realizing this beautiful catalogue and for its cooperation in the following award publications.

And, finally, our special thanks go to our 2023 finalists, who gave interviews and made their projects available for this catalogue. You are important role models for the next generation of women architects. DIVIA is very proud about its contribution to more equality, diversity, respect, and recognition in the field of architecture.

Diversity is not about the others; diversity is about you!

Editorial

Our motivation in founding the nonprofit Diversity in Architecture was to promote inclusivity and diversity in the architectural world. As a first step toward achieving this goal, we aim to increase the profile of committed, talented women with integrity in architecture.

Having existed for decades, the socially and structurally deep-rooted view that practicing architects are male must be replaced with a different image to ensure a more equal working environment in the sector. Even more importantly, we need to open up new horizons and identify role models to empower other generations of architects.

Today, in 2023, an equal proportion of male and female architecture students in the Western architectural profession are enrolled at universities. In some cases, women students are even in the majority. However, after their architectural education, they are faced with a daily working life for which these women were neither prepared nor trained: structural discrimination, bias, tasks that have little to do with what they have learned at university, working hours that prevent a balanced life outside architecture, and, finally, the incompatibility of parenthood and childcare with the career of an architect. One's intrinsic self-understanding is confronted by invisible manifestos. In the Western architectural industry, only around ten percent of female architects run their own studios, while fewer than thirty percent work in managerial positions.

And yet, they really do exist: self-employed women architects who conceive and build architecture in a bold, intelligent, and holistic way, despite the unfavorable conditions, thereby making their mark and developing their own architectural character. In doing so, they specifically apply subtle measures to address continental challenges, using both gentle and robust means, combined with the skill and passion to create a naturally constructed building, seemingly without any effort.

So why found an organization, why establish another award, why choose the label Diversity in Architecture?

Because we need role models!

We initially started by focusing on women architects, joining forces with eight eloquent and diverse personalities to found a platform on which we could operate. The award is an instrument with which to achieve visibility and provide financial support to as yet (mostly) unknown, talented women architects. A targeted press campaign and a touring exhibition with an accompanying publication provide lasting documentation, thereby also helping to increase the profiles of these architects. The *disappearance* of women architects and the inability to retrace them since the nineteen-twenties makes it more difficult to rewrite history. With a very few exceptions, they cannot be found because their work has hardly ever been documented, leading to a lack of sources. Even Le Corbusier failed to mention Eileen Gray and appropriated her work as late as 1946.

The methodology at DIVIA in announcing its diversity award is holistic: the advisory board consists of select experts with a grasp of their country, continent, professional sector, specific building tasks, and the typical state of the art technologies available in their countries. The board selects nominees, from which the equally excellent and diverse prize jury chooses five finalists for the award. The jury carries out the process internally every two years. In 2023, it consists of Sol Camacho from São Paulo, Odile Decq from Paris, Martha Thorne from Madrid, and Raul Mehrotra from Mumbai. In 2025, it will be supplemented by Itohan Osayimwese from Providence.

This publication is dedicated to the five finalists, who were interviewed and whose works and careers studied, as well as all the nominees and supporters of DIVIA. The catalogue is intended to accompany the exhibition, providing insight into the characters and working methods of prizewinning architects from Egypt, the United Kingdom, Nigeria, Peru, and Rwanda.

Today's global building tasks are unthinkable without resource-saving building, reuse concepts, and a holistic planning culture. The existing social framework should be widened and professional limitations challenged to enhance opportunities for women of all backgrounds, since their valuable perspectives enrich and open up new fields of activity. What we need now is the loyalty of male architects who have hitherto established and shaped the status quo. We invite you to act as examples in working together with younger generations on an equal footing, allowing their background and identity to play an enhancing role, in which integrity and skill are the decisive factors.

This year's DIVIA architects inspire us with their architectural gems, for which we thank them!

Jury's Preface

With the enormous amount of architecture awards today, which are constantly increasing, the question is: Why *divia award*? Is another prize, this time for women, really necessary? The founders have said: "The goal is to make women architects visible, to recognize and honor their work, to promote equality between male and female architects, and to raise awareness of role models for young women architects." However, the award goes well beyond this to embrace the diversity of geographic regions, approaches, organizations, and philosophies of professional work. In the future, I can imagine that the concept of diversity that DIVIA recognizes will evolve and reward other underrepresented and valuable participants in the creation of our built environment.

"Business as usual" is not an option, neither for women, the profession, nor the planet. Opening up our understanding of the built environment, those who participate in creating and constructing it, and its many impacts on how we live is imperative. Fostering talent, new knowledge, and an understanding of all members of society cannot be achieved if a male, Western minority dominates architecture and urban planning, as well as other adjacent industries, such as finance, construction, real estate, and building materials.

The jury of the *divia award* is charged with the decision of selecting a winner. This is no easy task, considering the talented women across the globe in the field of architecture and the broader field of urban planning. However, it is a most enjoyable and important task. The 2023 jury of four members, accompanied on its journey by many more—advisors, ambassadors, trustees, and the founders of the award—must make clear the criteria upon which the selection is made. Architecture is a changing field, not only because of the greater diversity of those who practice it, but because of changing definitions, responsibilities, and even the structure of firms and the roles that they develop. Social responsibility, caring for the natural environment, and creating buildings, spaces, and cities that can change and adapt to the evolving needs of our society is a far cry from the static image, devoid of people, to immortalize the opening of a building that architects often preferred in the past (and too many still value).

As a jury, we try to set aside our biases and find common ground that reflects excellence, talent, and, above all, professionals of high integrity that represent a true promise for the future. Not all women practice in the same way, nor within the same context. It is important to understand the milieu to empathize with women who have had to make a huge effort to get ahead, despite the circumstances. To chart a way ahead, our finalists have had to forge new paths. Innovation, or daring to do things differently in favor of the individual, community, and planet, is recognized by the jury. And, finally, we consider impact, which is of course a multifaceted concept. Yet, architecture that points the way to a more humane, sustainable, and meaningful environment is a beacon and inspiration for others. It is a way to share knowledge across the miles. Buildings, spaces, and communities extend well beyond their physical boundaries and provide settings for life. The task at hand and for the future is to make sure that the environments in which we live are responsible, sustainable, beautiful, humane, and meaningful. The finalists are all winners because they do this, creating paths that bring us together while still celebrating our individuality.

Members of the Jury

Sol Camacho is the cofounder of the architectural practice RADDAR, the former director of the Instituto Bardi/Casa de Vidro and coordinator of the Archive Lina Bo Bardi in São Paulo. Dedicated to a wide range of activities related to promoting the value of architecture for contemporary society, she works at the interface of practice and research.

Odile Decq runs her eponymously named studio in Paris with a multidisciplinary approach. In 2014, she founded the alternative architecture school Confluence Institute for Innovation and Creative Strategies in Architecture. In 2016, she won the Jane Drew Prize for raising the recognition of women in architecture.

Rahul Mehrotra is the founding principal of RMA Architects, whose focus lies on the "creation of awareness of architecture" in India. Based between Mumbai and Boston, he is Professor of Urban Design and Planning and the John T. Dunlop Professor in Housing and Urbanization at Harvard University.

Martha Thorne is the former executive director of the Pritzker Architecture Prize and currently the dean of IE School of Architecture & Design in Madrid. As such, she strives to bring the best of innovation and management to architectural disciplines. She was also the initiator and presenter of the manifesto "Voices of Women" at the Venice Architecture Biennale in 2018.

Jury's Statement

she has embraced under the umbrella of architecture as a way of serving a broad array of constituencies in society.

We congratulate Marta Maccaglia on winning the first *divia award* and wish the four finalists all the best in their future endeavors.

The jury gathered on March 25, 2023, at Aedes in Berlin to select the winner of the *divia award* 2023. Martha Thorne and Odile Decq were present in person, Sol Camacho and Rahul Mehrotra joined via Zoom.

An objective of the *divia award* is to expand the definition of architectural practice, realizing that there are many ways to undertake the profession. Therefore, we would like to recognize the broad spectrum of work of the five professionals, represented by the different modes each of them uses to approach and engage with society. All five finalists reflect a commitment to the broader challenges for the profession of architecture and design today, and they do this in generous, creative, and thoughtful ways. We also celebrate the forms of patronage that they embrace.

We chose Marta Maccaglia as the winner because we were impressed with the consistency of her architectural attitude to her projects, from small to large scale, while every project is also reflective of the local culture and the particularities of the place. Working in underserved geographies, she creates buildings that can respond to the dynamic needs of the community with a generous spirit, humanist approach, and courageous attitude. Since coming to Peru, Marta Maccaglia has become part of her adoptive country as an equal. In 2014, she founded the NGO Semillas to be more critically and cooperatively embedded in the local context and to help in understanding local materials.

We celebrate May al-Ibrashy's tenacity and dedication to the restoration of cultural heritage within Historic Cairo. She is a talented designer and a valuable enabler of education, conservation, and community cohesion. She embodies architecture as a cultural practice for helping people and succeeds in constructing an ecology of activities that make the built environment more sustainable.

Katherine Clarke and Liza Fior use a multidisciplinary approach to architecture in public spaces based on the idea that architecture is a catalyst to create forms of inclusive environments. Their practice muf architecture/art activates public spaces and, in the process, enables new relationships within communities.

After studying in South Africa, Noella Nibakuze returned to her home country of Rwanda and joined the NPO Mass Design Group—a model of a collective organization that produces architecture for the underserved. She shows the importance of participating in a collective and collaborative work configuration and highlights the significance of a trajectory of practice within an organizational platform.

Tosin Oshinowo demonstrates the diversity of modes of engagement, from curation to infrastructural design. We would like to acknowledge the wide range of activities that

9 Winner

10 Marta Maccaglia

Finalists

26 May Al-Ibrashy

42 Katherine Clarke & Liza Fior

58 Noella Nibakuze

74 Tosin Oshinowo

Marta Maccaglia

The rainforest is a place full of culture and tradition that is often overlooked. The Italian architect Marta Maccaglia set out to protect it. After studying interior architecture and exhibition design in Italy, she moved to Peru in 2011 to gain practical experience and participate in an international cooperation program. Only three years later, she founded Semillas, a nonprofit architectural organization with an "Amazonian heart and spirit," whose aim is to put emphasis on territories that are usually ignored. Based in Pangoa, Lima, and San Ignacio, it is run by an interdisciplinary team of architects, builders, and artisans. Together, they create and execute educational architecture projects and public spaces by collaborating with governmental, nongovernmental, and educational entities. Semillas see their practice as a cultural expression, taking into consideration the voices of Indigenous communities in all stages of the process. They believe that cooperative work is the only way to forge development and create a strong foundation of opportunities. Therefore, territorial and societal knowledge is a prerequisite for creating spaces in architecture that are in harmony with the soul of each location. With thirteen completed projects to date, each one was born out of a collaborative way of working, based on a deep understanding of its users in their social and economic context.

Born in 1983 in Italy
Established her architectural association Semillas in 2014
Based in Lima, Peru
www.semillasperu.com

"I see education as the main tool for freedom. If we want a better society, we need an educated population."

The Italian architect Marta Maccaglia came to Peru in 2011 through an Italian government program. Fresh out of university, she expected to work as a teacher in a nursery in Huaycán but instead encountered ruins where there should have been a building. Faced with two options, either to leave or to stay, she chose the latter. With zero practical experience and only the help of a local NGO, she built the nursery from the ground up within six months.

Over a decade later, Marta Maccaglia is still in Peru, now leading her organization Semillas that builds schools and public spaces in the most remote areas of the Peruvian jungle. Her work has been celebrated with numerous awards, including the 2018 Global Award for Sustainable Architecture. Veronika Lukashevich met her via Skype to speak about her approach to working closely with the communities, the current political climate in Peru, and creating inviting classrooms for children and teachers. They were also joined by Marta's colleague and architect Giulia Perri.

Veronika   Building a nursery with few resources is a huge endeavor and requires a lot of imagination.
Marta   I learned it from my mom. When I was little, she used to create games and houses for my dolls using only recycled materials. She could make beautiful things from nothing and without any money, so, in a way, it is part of my approach. When I was in secondary school I participated in a competition to design the courtyard for our school and won. The courtyard had looked so limited, so I included some trees and a bench into my design to make it look more comfortable. Later, I studied exhibition design for my master's degree. A museum is an expression of a moment of history, so, to me, exhibition spaces are linked with educational spaces. I see education as the main tool for freedom. If we want a better society, we need an educated population. Currently, Peru's impoverished population is marching the streets demanding reform. The repressed groups are constantly fighting for their freedom of expression and basic rights, namely access to education, health care, and public infrastructure.
Veronika   How do you see diversity and multiculturalism in Peru within the framework of your work?
Marta   Peru is a multicultural and diverse country. There are three micro-regions, namely *costa* (coast), *sierra* (mountains), and *selva* (rainforest), and we have forty-eight native languages, different Indigenous communities with their own customs and ways of thinking. So, the diversity of Peru has

great potential, but it can also become a problem. People are still dealing with trauma caused by the Spanish colonization, which is palpable in the entire country. The government tries to unify the country with their policies, disregarding the different identities, which is ultimately reflected in the architectural model that aims to replicate European modernism. But the Peruvian mindset is different. This is why it is so important to become a part of the place and the people's way of living before you start building. Semillas cooperates using a participatory approach based on dialogue. For us, the way to build common spaces is through respecting this diversity that encompasses the people's cultural wealth, rights, and knowledge. We believe that cooperation is a possible dream and the only way.
Veronika   You studied in Europe. In what way did you have to adjust your way of working to the rural environment in the Peruvian jungle?
Marta   What I value about my education is the tools to research, listen, and observe. But when I arrived in Peru, my architectural knowledge was not relevant to local buildings and local customs. Usually, Latin American cities are surrounded by human settlements, which have been built by the dwellers themselves, without architects. In Peru, the way people make cities is through *faenas* (communal work), meaning people work together for a common purpose.
Giulia   The people who live in the forest or in a rural area are used to creating their own houses and spaces; they are more active in that sense. For example, putting up a column of wood helps them develop a connection to the spaces, and they become a part of it. It is not just the process of design that is important but also the process of making and capturing their identity through these spaces.
Marta   With Semillas, our impact has three different layers. Firstly, we conceptualize infrastructure not only as a physical space but as a symbol of opportunity and equality, especially since a school is usually the only public building in the rural community. Secondly, our impact lies in improving the empirical communitarian process and taking it to a new participatory level as a learning process of interchange. A space where everyone can participate actively in the decision-making. The third layer of impact is rescuing the millenary knowledge and revaluing. It is about revendicating the social habitat and well-being of each society. We research the territory, the people, and their history. All parties take an opportunity to reflect: the school, the community, the parents, the

architects, the local government. But it is important to mention that our step-by-step methodology is only a guideline, and we carefully adapt it with every project. It is a constant process—freeing ourselves from our own prejudices.

Veronika   The native communities in the jungle have experienced violence in the past, and still do. What does this mean in terms of your approach?

Marta   Gaining trust is a gradual process, too. Usually, when outsiders, politicians, or NGOs arrive in the community, they make promises, but they do very little and only stay for a fixed period of time. In our case, we are a family. As soon as the local people understood that we do not have any economic interests, they began to trust us. I am not a charitable Italian lady—we exchange knowledge and gain something from these experiences because we learn about their culture, and they learn about ours. Another important aspect is that we involve local policy since our projects are funded through international cooperation and the local government. We designed a management system in which the forces from the local and external institutions are joined.

Veronika   Could you give an example of how you include the community in the decision-making process?

Marta   To ensure that we respond to the community's needs, we hold meetings and participatory workshops with the communities for the whole duration of the project. At the beginning, we do not talk about the appearance of the space but focus on finding out the feeling that they look for and the activities that they want to do in these spaces. For example, the teachers might want to play ancestral games with the students or teach them about medicinal plants and agricultural issues. After they have shared their ideas, we start to reflect on how the spaces can support these activities.

Giulia   In the process of building a nursery for fifty children and a community space for the Nomatsiguenga people in Alto Anapati, the teachers explained to us how they usually need a moment during the day to tell tales in the classroom. We took the time to observe them in this activity: the teacher sat in front of the class while the children were seated on the floor encircling the teacher. For the stories that were being told, it was important that the forest remained the backdrop, so we were sure to include a big window in the back.

Marta   For this project, we also built an outdoor learning space called *aula bosque* (forest classroom). We had asked the teachers what their ideal classroom looked like, and they imagined a tree in the middle of the space with a little fence around it. This created a place for the children and the teachers to learn in harmony with nature. We also included big sliding doors to connect interior spaces with the forest. In terms of building and construction, we reinterpret and revalue local materials to create a more familiar atmosphere. In the Alto Anapati school, the objects that the community uses in their daily lives became a part of the design. For example, a basket to transport yuca, wood, or agricultural products was used to create lamps. The tapestries, made from palm trees, that the Nomatsiguenga use for sleeping or eating, were used as walls. Schools built by the government, on the other hand, are concrete bunkers. They are surrounded by tall fences, and the classrooms have high windows so that children do not get distracted. The architecture does not reflect the people's needs to bring their identity, culture, and nature together. With Semillas, we try to create free and open spaces by breaking down barriers.

Veronika   I imagine the feedback from the children must be very heartwarming.

Marta   When asked what they liked about their school, one of them said: "It has the color of my skin and my *cushma*" [the tunic worn by the native communities]. It is a source of great pride for us to see how architecture, aesthetics, form, and color create an atmosphere and a place that emanates freedom and identification.

Veronika   What is next for Semillas?

Marta   I see our organization continuing to develop educational, communitarian, exhibition, and cultural projects in Peru and abroad while having political impact on housing policies. I also see us sharing our experience and knowledge through workshops at international universities and having a multiplier effect on architectural pedagogy at a global scale.

Nursery School, Alto Anapati

Year   2019–21
Funding   Fly & Help and Municipalidad de Pangoa

Alto Anapati is situated in Pangoa in the middle of the Peruvian jungle. Characterized by poverty and poor infrastructure, it is the home to 455 people from the Nomatsiguenga ethnic community. To strengthen the right of children to a good education and improve their quality of learning, Semillas built a 397-square-meter school for ninety children consisting of various spaces. The building is located in the access area to the community and is organized in two blocks. The block on the southwest side contains the multipurpose room, the administrative area, the kitchen, and the toilets. The multipurpose room is directly connected to the *aula bosque* (forest classroom)—an area designed as an outdoor classroom. The classroom block on the east side opens to outdoor areas through large sliding partitions. Most of the materials used in the project were locally sourced, including wood, clay bricks, and river stones. The process was carried out through participatory workshops, which led to the creation of the concept: making the school the heart of the community and a place where Nomatsiguenga knowledge and territory can be preserved.

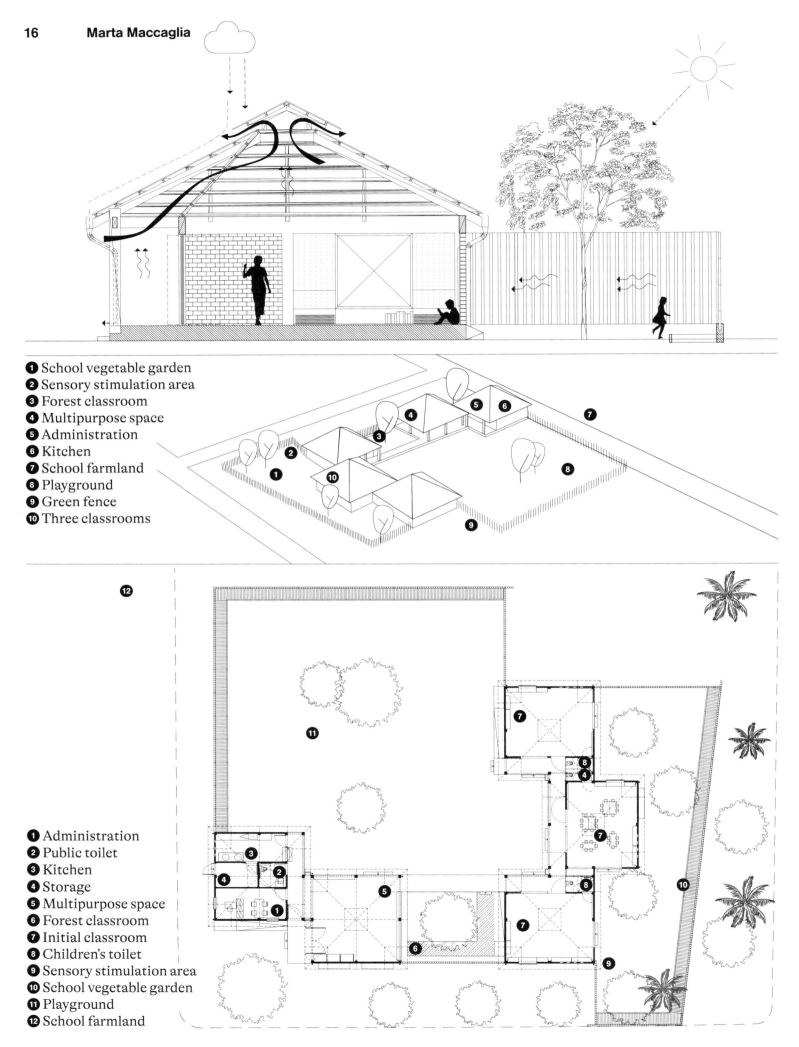

1 School vegetable garden
2 Sensory stimulation area
3 Forest classroom
4 Multipurpose space
5 Administration
6 Kitchen
7 School farmland
8 Playground
9 Green fence
10 Three classrooms

1 Administration
2 Public toilet
3 Kitchen
4 Storage
5 Multipurpose space
6 Forest classroom
7 Initial classroom
8 Children's toilet
9 Sensory stimulation area
10 School vegetable garden
11 Playground
12 School farmland

Primary School, Jerusalén De Miñaro

Year 2017
Funding Costa Foundation

The school is located in the native community of Jerusalen de Miñaro, in the central jungle of Peru. Based on participatory research, the process was the foundation for the exchange of knowledge and experience, which resulted in 1,000 square meters of construction and 269 square meters of remodeling space. Semillas followed a bioclimatic design using local resources and creating versatile spaces that inspire freedom and creativity. The corridors and patios connected to the classrooms form circuits and routes of play. The wooden divisions can be used as hiding places and the windows as chairs. The multifunctional module and the patios can be adapted for various activities such as community meetings, parties, and public and sports events. The school offers educational spaces and serves as a social catalyst, creating opportunities for all.

1 Sanitary facilities
Improvement of lavatories
for students and teachers
2 Parque Bambú
children's playground
3 Block 3
Two classrooms
One covered courtyard

4 Block 2
Three classrooms
One covered courtyard
5 Block 1
Three classrooms
One covered courtyard

6 Multifuncional Block 4
Main entrance, hall,
cafeteria, multipurpose room,
kitchen, computer room,
storage shed, sanitary
facilities
7 Children's playground
Football courtyard

8 Existing building
We propose to convert this
infrastructure to
a teacher dormitory and an
administrative office

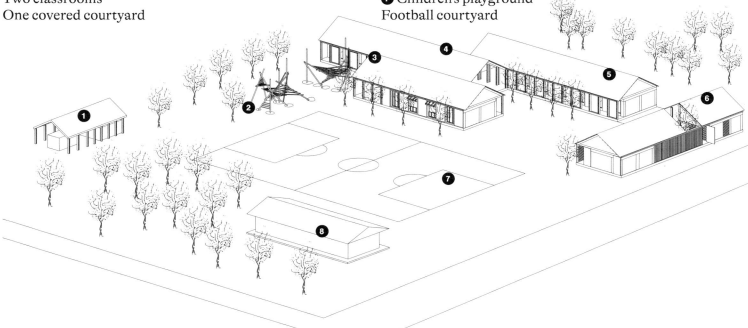

1 Main access
2 Canteen
3 Small canteen
4 Kitchen
5 Warehouse Qali Wuarma

6 Bathrooms
7 Storage for sports
equipment/changing room
8 Computer room/multi-
functional

9 Vegetable garden
10 Classrooms
11 Covered patio
12 Open patio
13 Reforestation area

14 Parque Bambù
15 Vehicular access

Community Center, Otica

Year   2019
Funding   NEMATSA SRL, Native Community of
           Otica

Otica's Asháninka community is located on the banks of the Tambo River in the central jungle of Peru. Since the previous community center provided by the local government had gone into a state of disuse due to the lack of cultural and environmental comfort, Semillas created a 230-square-meter gathering space according to the needs of the community. For this they used the wood from the Otica forest, the stones from the nearby river, and the clay bricks from the neighboring communities. The center is a focal point of the community, attached to the main square and the soccer field. The building consists of a strip foundation of stone and cement that rises from the ground to protect against flooding. Simultaneously, it works as a grandstand, opening up toward the exterior and the interior, generating a space in the shape of a rectangular amphitheater. The wooden portico supports a gabled roof of fiber cement sheets. Two access plazas, equipped with a bench on their border and a native tree in the middle, indicate the accesses to the local communal space. To the north, a concrete and brick module contains the kitchen, office, and craft workshop, which unfolds on two levels.

❶ Community area: square, theater, dining room, conference room
❷ Exterior corridors
❸ Stage
❹ Office
❺ Kitchen
❻ Bleachers seats
❼ Access square

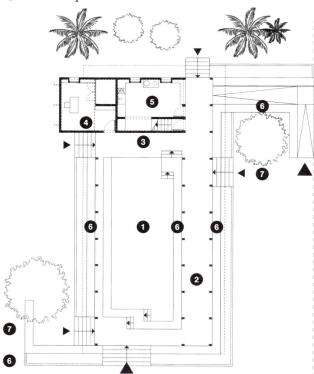

Nursery and Primary School, Unión Alto Sanibeni

Year   2019
Funding   Costa Foundation

The school is located in the native Asháninka community of Unión Alto Sanibeni in Pangoa, Peru. In the nineties, this region was depopulated due to Peru's internal armed conflict. The community returned after 1998 but lived in abandonment for twenty years. In addition to serving 200 children from the community, the school benefits more than 1,000 inhabitants of the region. Encompassing 1,200 square meters, the school consists of three corridors underneath a large roof, and the layout is distributed around a multipurpose area (the plaza). It includes six classrooms for primary education and two for nursery school, bathrooms with changing rooms, storage rooms, a kitchen, and a library. In the classrooms, the walls are used as bookshelves and teaching surfaces. Two wide hallways run through the building with views of the countryside and connect to the large central plaza. In the common spaces, all the surfaces are designed for teaching: the colorful wooden panels along the walls, for example, can be folded down into tables. The exterior walls are brick made from heated clay, a commonly used material and a locally made product.

May Al-Ibrashy

May al-Ibrashy's work within cultural heritage and conservation of Historic Cairo revolutionizes the idea of what might traditionally fall under the idea of practicing architecture as a profession. After studying archaeology, conservation, and art history, she first worked as an architect and professor, then created Megawra (Neighborhood) at the end of 2011. The nonprofit architectural office runs in partnership with the Built Environment Collective (BEC), a local cultural and urban development organization. It is a place where cultural heritage is seen as a driver for progress—a key factor for changing societies and creating urban development on the community's terms. One of Megawra's main initiatives is Athar Lina (The monument is ours), a participatory conservation project that kicked off in 2012. Grounded in the idea that heritage is a resource and not a burden, it aims to ignite the relationship between people and their heritage by encouraging the local Egyptian communities to become cocreators of their city. Through her work, May al-Ibrashy has positively impacted the impoverished groups living in Cairo's historic center. She has also introduced a different narrative to the government's fixation on urban expansion and renewal, developing a new sense of ownership for the impacted communities.

Born in 1969 in Egypt
Established her NPO-BEC Megawra in 2011
Based in Cairo, Egypt
www.atharlina.com
www.megawra.com

"The meanings tend to be unlike what is written in the description of these monuments. They are in the myths, the family histories."

Fair-like festivities play out in the streets of Old Cairo, as crowds of people from all over Egypt are gathered for the Mawlid al-Husayn, the birthday celebration of the grandson of the Islamic prophet Muhammad. It is the year 1989, and Egyptian architect and engineer-in-training May al-Ibrashy is working on the conservation of al-Harrawi House, an eighteenth-century Ottoman residential building. The interior atmosphere does not match the bustling energy of the chaos happening outside these building's walls. It is quiet, grand—a mixture of serenity and sublime beauty within a frenzied environment. But May al-Ibrashy does not find this kind of contradiction unsettling. On the contrary: it makes her fall in love with Historic Cairo in the first place.

"There is a surprise around every corner," she says. "And that, for me, is wonderful and continues to be so. These interactions between the communities and the buildings that are from hundreds of years ago—somehow they fit, they have grown well together."

As May al-Ibrashy daydreams of her student days in Cairo, she finds herself in her hotel room in Charlotte, North Carolina, where the previous day she held a presentation at the University of North Carolina at Charlotte. Veronika Lukashevich met her via Zoom in early February 2023 to speak about how her work in conservation has developed over the last thirty-plus years.

In 2011, May al-Ibrashy cofounded Megawra—Built Environment Collective, a partnership between an NGO and an architectural practice, specializing in conservation and heritage management. It was originally created as a coworking space for architects, academics, and urbanists in Heliopolis, serving as a cultural place mainly for students who were looking for input from other disciplines. This "quest inward," as May al-Ibrashy calls it, was happening at a very uncertain time in her country whose future was marked by the 2011 Egyptian revolution.

May   It was a moment of great fluidity for the entire city. Everyone was soul-searching, and there was an openness from the governmental stakeholders that I do not think you will find today because their sense of who they were had been dismantled by the revolution. In 2012, we investigated the question of ownership of heritage through stakeholder workshops and participatory research in al-Khalifa, the southern section of Historic Cairo. Because this area is very close to the cemetery, it has a string of shrines along the street, which were not well taken care of, so we saw a lot of potential for conservation work there. The communities that live in the area are very impoverished, but the atmosphere is warm, strong, and vibrant, unlike other places of Historic Cairo that either have become more of a tourist bubble or commercial with warehouses and shops. As we began working on conservation projects, we created the Athar Lina initiative. As it grew, we moved our office to al-Khalifa in 2014 to continue our work in the neighborhood.

Veronika   How would you describe the relationship between the communities in al-Khalifa and their heritage?

May   There are many layers to this relationship. Sometimes there is a disconnect that has come about because of years of a policy that attempts to protect the buildings by separating them from the community by building fences, controlling access, changing the function of the building. But what is amazing is that beneath the surface, you find layers and layers of connections that are generational. And you cannot just get rid of them. The meanings that you find tend to be unlike what you are taught in the history books or what is written in the description of these monuments. They are in the myths, the family histories—this is what we tend to work with more.

Veronika   What were some of the other results of your research?

May   Conservation is important, but you have to think of the use of the building after the conservation project is complete and how it can benefit the community. We also noticed very early on that the younger the residents, the less connected they are to the heritage sites. We felt that it was probably because these sites had become so inaccessible that the children never even entered these buildings. This is how our heritage education programs came about. With them, we aim to foster a sense of ownership of heritage at a young age. Another question that unfolded was about how to ground these limited actions within a wider urban setting. What kind of urban regeneration, socioeconomic development, and environmental improvement do we need to make the area a better place for the people and for these heritage sites?

Veronika   You have completed five conservation projects to date, yet the mausoleum of Imam Shafi'i is your favorite. What makes it so special?

May   It took six years to finish, so it is our biggest conservation project in terms of size and importance. The mosque is a record of the decorative styles in the Islamic period from the twelfth century onward. We developed a technique to fix the marble cladding mechanically, resolved structural issues of subsidence and active cracks, and resolved issues with the lead cladding of the dome itself. Because of climate change, we have different rain patterns now, so we were dealing with more intense rain-related damage leading to leakage into the building. On the exterior, it was the conservation of the stucco and making sure that everything is well consolidated without making the building look new. The interior is painted, so we had to peel down the layers of overpaint from the previous conservation projects to figure out the original color palette. Through a major excavation project, we also discovered an older shrine that had existed an entire century prior to this one, so we decided to install a visitor's center to share all the new information. The dome is also a place of spirituality. One of the most beautiful rituals is that Egyptians write letters to the Imam and put them in the shrine. There is a beautiful aura to that place that goes beyond anything physical.

Veronika   What educational programs do you run within heritage education?

May   During the conservation work, we will typically run heritage education activities for the residents to teach them more about the building and the work that we do. We also run an annual summer school for two months and a vocational education program, in which we introduce young people to the variety of career opportunities within heritage. We train about twenty to thirty interns per year through extensive lectures, discussions, readings, and on the job training. We started off with the children but then got to know their mothers, too. At some point they asked us: "Why don't you run something for us?" So, naturally, we expanded the scope of our work. We included the component of heritage industries, where the women create products related to heritage, and we offer them for sale. We are also currently in the process of setting up a small workshop for textile crafts, which should employ around twelve women.

Veronika   Can you speak about how you include the women in the process of designing their neighborhoods through storytelling? I find this approach highly compelling.

May   The engagement with the women is important because they have become important partners in our decision-making process. We conduct needs assessments directly through consultation meetings but also indirectly through a storytelling program. A professional storyteller leads long and confidential sessions with the women to explore their relationship to their neighborhood. It tends to be an empowering experience because it is a rendition of their history as opposed to the bigger histories that people know of the neighborhood. Some of the topics discussed in the sessions are issues concerning safety or the perception of green areas. These are people who have been subjected to years of poorly maintained open spaces, so, for example, there is a worry concerning who will take ownership of these areas. They cannot be left open because the strongest group within the community will just take over. There is this constant questioning of our own preconceptions.

Veronika   Athar Lina is mainly led by a female team. How important is it to have a close-knit women's community within an initiative to help build and enable strong and resilient societies?

May   I like to support women in practical ways, in making sure I am not being discriminatory in the kinds of jobs that are assigned, as well as being open to flexible hours and bringing children to work. However, in places like Egypt, we focus so much on gender that we do not notice the class issues as much. These issues are more endemic and more problematic. People who work in architecture tend to be of the upper middle class, so we are trying to be as diverse as possible where class is concerned. We also ask ourselves: What principles and ethos are we projecting through our work in terms of messaging? Like I said, it is also about the smaller narratives and histories that write the city through everyday life.

Veronika   You have been working within the realms of conservation for over thirty years. How has the people's relationship to heritage changed over time in Egypt?

May   Today, there are more people working within heritage or showing interest in it, going on tours, or just visiting the neighborhoods. Unfortunately, the reason for this is quite sad because a lot of these sites have been under threat. Various urban development projects have been happening on the peripheries of the city in the last few years, the most important one being the new administrative capital. There is this constant feeling of losing something, so the people are becoming more invested. It is bittersweet.

Veronika   You are currently working on an educational platform with a group of international and local partners.

May   Yes, together with two other firms we want to develop a platform that consolidates the knowledge that we have generated for people who want to work in the built environment. It is not about focusing on construction but on improving what exists. Architects need to start thinking about complex engagements with the built environment that are less extractive and more responsible, socially and environmentally. This requires a team of different disciplines. Architects tend to think that they can do this alone, but there are skills that are needed from other disciplines.

Veronika   You are trying to diversify the idea of architecture.

May   For years, people have said to me: "You are an architect, so why are you doing this work?" Students would want to intern with us, but their professors would advise against it because we are not an architecture firm. But there are many ways of practicing architecture. I think it starts with being very mindful of how you operate and what your strengths are and then building on that.

Al-Imam al-Shafi'i Dome

Year   2016–21
Client   Egyptian Ministry of Tourism and Antiquities

Imam al-Shafi'i was the founder of the Shafi'i school of Sunni jurisprudence. Dating back to the twelfth century, the mausoleum is one of the most important Islamic landmarks and, with an internal diameter of 15.3 meters, the largest wooden dome in Egypt. Situated in al-Khalifa in Historic Cairo, it is emblematic of several different eras of Islamic art. The conservation was completed in two phases. The first round focused on the conservation of the dome exterior, including stucco, lead cladding, and metal boat finial, as well as masonry and roof repair, conservation of wooden elements, mosaic floor, and marble cladding and excavation and repair of subsidence problems. The second round dealt with the conservation works in the entrance and the corridor to the mosque, as well as the dome interior, including carved stucco windows, painted wood decoration on the interior surface of the dome, and conservation of the wooden doors and windows. The third phase involved the installation of a visitor's center in a nineteenth-century building adjacent to the shrine. The project was funded by the US Ambassador's Fund for Cultural Preservation and included additional funding from the US Embassy in Cairo, the Barakat Trust, UK, the Embassy of the Netherlands in Cairo, the Prince Claus Fund, and the ALIPH Foundation.

Mausoleum of al-Imam al-Shafi'i
Exterior East Elevation

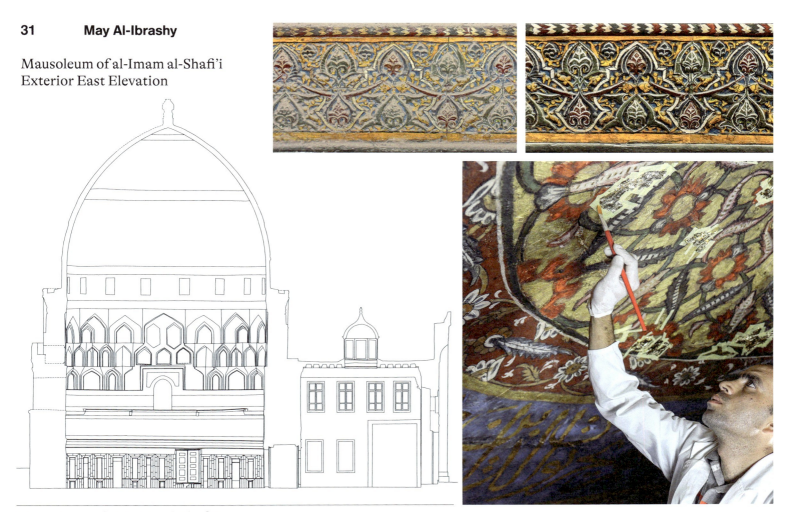

Mausoleum of al-Imam al-Shafi'i
Ground floor plan

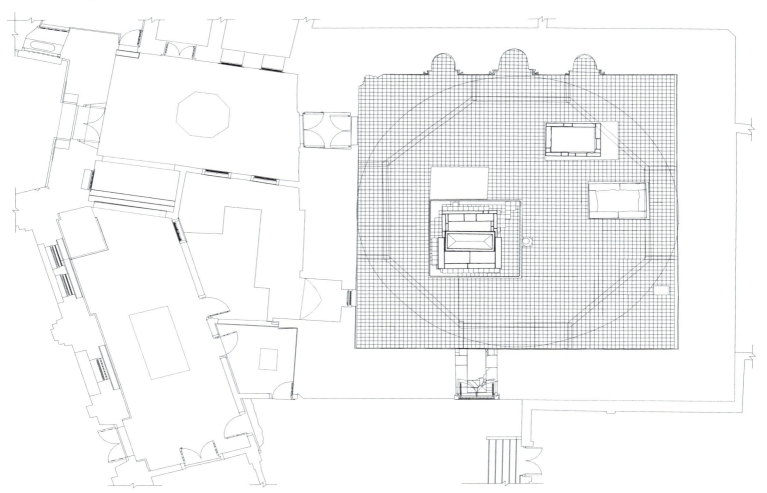

Al-Khalifa Park

Year 2017–ongoing
Client Cairo Governorate

Located in al-Khalifa, Historic Cairo, the 3,000-square-meter park is the result of Athar Lina's Groundwater Research Project and their initiative to create more green spaces and recreational spaces in the area. An irrigation system was designed for the park, reusing more than seventy percent of ground and subsurface water inundating the neighboring domes. It is a step toward social and economic development and raising the standard of living in the area. Through needs assessments, field studies, and participatory workshops, Athar Lina determined women and children as the main target. The park's southern section highlights a children's playground, an open theater, green spaces, an urban farming section, and waste collection points. The northern section is yet to be implemented and should include a women's sports area, a kindergarten, restaurants, cafés, and shops. The implementation of the project was funded by the Cairo Governorate and the Embassy of the Netherlands in Cairo. The design and research were funded by the Ford Foundation, the American Research Center in Egypt, the US Embassy in Cairo, the Prince Claus Fund for Culture and Development, and the US Forest Service.

Khalifa Heritage and Environment park

Extraction using underground perforated pipes

Sedimentation and pump station

Pumping water to the park

Water storage tank and park irrigation system

1. Urban farming educational center
2. Women's sports center
3. Kindergarten
4. Storytelling and playground
5. Main plaza
6. Ramp from al-Khalifa to neighbouring district
7. Cafeteria
8. Forest
9. Shops
10. Garbage collection points
11. Water storage tank

إعادة استخدام المياه الأرضية في متنزه الخليفة
Irrigating al-Khalifa Park with groundwater

تلف الآثار بسبب الرطوبة و الأملاح
Salt and damp damage buildings

تتسرب المياه من الشبكات و تتلوث بالأملاح
Water leaks from networks and collects salts

سحب المياه من أسفل الآثار و استخدامها لري متنزه الخليفة
Groundwater is collected from under monuments and used to irrigate al-Khalifa Park

Al-Hattaba Masterplan

Year   2018–ongoing
Client   Egyptian Ministry of Tourism and Antiquities

The al-Hattaba neighborhood is a representative example of Historic Cairo's urban fabric. The BEC's vision for the project is to revitalize the rundown buildings and turn them into new spaces. The aim is to elevate al-Hattaba as a historical area that is easy to develop as a crafts and tourism neighborhood. The master plan addresses three developmental areas: touristic heritage with a focus on establishing a tourist route, crafts targeting the creation of new workshops and centers for design (see the crafts center on page 38), as well as the rehabilitation of residential buildings and emprovement of public spaces. Athar Lina is currently developing the preliminary plan into a more extensive study to be taken into consideration within the Egyptian government's vision for the regeneration of Historic Cairo. The project is funded by the Ford Foundation.

One of the advocacy components in the al-Hattaba development program was the project "Women Quilt for Al-Hattaba" (see page 39) that tried to showcase the history of the neighborhood in a creative way. The women from the local community were joined by a designer and a *khiyamiyya* (patchwork) artisan to create a communal *khiyamiyya* quilt that tells the history of al-Hattaba from their perspective.

Heritage Education

The Heritage Education Program is rooted in the idea that heritage and monuments belong to everyone—when people learn their value, their desire to preserve them for future generations is stronger. Encompassing this concept is the annual Khalifa Summer Camp (2014–ongoing). Taking place in the Al-Khalifa Community Center, an early twentieth-century building rehabilitated into a community space, it runs for free for the children in al-Khalifa. The idea is to support them in developing a sense of ownership of their heritage through art, sports, crafts, and other activities. Another seminal project within Heritage Education is the Athar Lina Heritage Design Thinking School (2018–22), which was funded by the Drosos Foundation. It was a three-year scheme that worked with craftspeople, designers, artists, as well as residents of al-Khalifa to transform its heritage into a contemporary line of products, services, and activities. The program has now progressed into the second phase, also funded by the Drosos Foundation, called Heritage Works (2023–26). It builds on the heritage industries and heritage education with women, youth, young adults, and craftspeople in al-Khalifa. While the first phase was centered on education and design development, the second phase is focused on economic empowerment. The Heritage Education component is also manifested in different forms in other projects. This includes heritage-inspired games and activity kits created for the visitor's center in al-Imam al-Shafi'i Dome (funded by different entities) and heritage-themed playdates for children in al-Khalifa.

Katherine Clarke & Liza Fior

Muf architecture/art is an internationally recognized practice that follows a transdisciplinary approach. Since its inception in 1995 in London, founding partners Katherine Clarke and Liza Fior, who met when they were both working at the Architectural Association, have worked with the intention of making genuine public space. Their projects range from urban design schemes to small-scale temporary interventions via landscapes and buildings—a constant dialogue between details and strategy. Always going beyond the job, artist Katherine Clarke and architect Liza Fior do not shy away from challenging a commission. Continuously with high standards for quality, their sustainable outcomes are based on social inclusion, regeneration, and legacy. With their primarily female studio, Katherine and Liza have worked on various projects, mainly in London and internationally, including urban strategies in the cities of Pittsburgh, Malmö, and Gothenburg. Every project is met with a great amount of research, interviews, and discussions with residents, users, developers, associations, and institutions, whose wishes are all presented in maps and diagrams. Simultaneously pragmatic and endlessly ambitious, they have pioneered methods of working directly with communities.

Katherine Clarke: born in 1961 in the United Kingdom
Liza Fior: born in 1962 in the United Kingdom
Established their studio muf architecture/art in 1995
Both based in London, United Kingdom
www.muf.co.uk

"We try not to spend time convincing the doubters; rather, we seek out and build coalitions with those who are not even yet part of the process."

Muf are a transdisciplinary art and architecture practice focused upon the public realm. They are renowned for their resolutely speculative approach to any commission. This requires perseverance with open-ended processes and the inclusion of the multiplicity of narratives that belong to a public space and its histories. In challenging both their clients and any attempted generic design agendas, muf's founding partners Katherine Clarke and Liza Fior embrace the complexity that is fundamental to an expanded field. Francesca Ferguson spoke to them via Zoom.

Francesca You are the finalists with the greatest longevity and pioneers of inclusive, participatory design for the public realm. What does diversity mean to you?

Katherine For us, diversity has always been about inclusion and finding out how to make a reading of a site that is accurate, so that it reflects the people who use it. By that I mean that it reflects the people who are marginalized from using it, who have an inequality of access or an inequality of need, and that it reflects how we try to make structures that include them. Although we have worked internationally, most of our work is in London, much in East London. It is always publicly accessible, if not publicly owned.

Liza It is particular to the fact that we have made that early commitment to only work in the public realm. For example, we declare that we are interested in the user as the client and not necessarily just the client commissioning. Diversity has to do with representation. It is about agency and seeing who is present. In that role as designers, we are making responses that are precise, when the avoidance of risk often tends towards the generic.

Francesca Looking back on your work, either a recent project or a seminal one, where have you turned into design the presence of previously unheard voices?

Liza The first project we did together was Southwark Street. It started with a video that brought all the different interests together. The video was publicly exhibited and, in that way, made the whole range of the client body public and visible, including, importantly, to each other.

Francesca How did this impact the design?

Katherine One of the benches we designed was on a school route. After speaking with the local children, we made a small child-height cutout into the bench to acknowledge how they perceive spaces. This is a direct struggle between research, inclusion, and design. There is a literal thread between these conversations and how they play out in a form or in a material.

Francesca You are also generating a completely different level of community action. It seems to me that whichever site you tackle, there is the galvanizing of a community.

Katherine For a project in Wood Green Common, we engaged in action research for a public commission to design an open green space. There were very vocal residents who lived on the Common; however, the voices of the Asian elders in the community were less amplified. We picked up on the tension between the younger and older generations. Because of street crime, older people were fearful of the young. There was mutual distrust. So, in a celebratory and rather theatrical way, we got the teenagers from the local school to host a tea party on the Common for the elders. Indian music was playing; it was a beautiful setting. In the end, over 1,000 teenagers walked past that scene. It was a way of making that potential to share visible. We were making room for more than one thing at a time.

Liza You start by valuing what is there, then you nurture the possible, and only then do you describe what is missing. You sort of put the wedge in the door. You have elbowed in the possibility of complexity. We had to hone our craft and our instincts on how to operate because we had to justify what we were doing. It has not been easy. These projects are over twenty-five years apart, but they are both about enactment and performance. They are about finding voices and making these different constituencies perform to each other.

Francesca What should diversity mean in order to resonate with our times of climate crisis and migration and the multiplicity of identities that belong to an urban realm?

Katherine The public realm is potentially the only space of well-being for those in precarious situations. It is also about the precarious state of nature, about making space for nature in the city. Biodiversity is measurable, and, to a certain extent, social value is measurable. But it depends on where you are measuring and where you put the base line. The impact extends longitudinally through a long period of time.

Liza It is important not just to perform diversity. It is about what and whom you include and the power you share. It requires making space for things that are not your cup of tea, are unknown, or uncomfortable. It starts by not being complacent in order to understand who and what is missing from the table, the brief, and the decision-making. It then requires you to work out what is needed to make that coming to the table possible.

Francesca Fundamentally, your work has a lot to do with excavating histories embedded in a site. You are also taking the challenge of staying within a local context and revisiting it.

Liza   To make the generic specific and appropriate to those who will use it requires unsolicited research, which is additional to a brief. Lived experience can and should shape future plans. Space should be made for such experience, whether it is in built form or a planning document that changes in terms of what it makes important: a tree gets more room to grow, for its roots to take up more ground.

Katherine Our art project Art Camp began as a reaction to the foreseeable impact of the heat of the post-2012 Olympic development on Hackney Wick and Fish Island, namely, what happens when there are no underdetermined, postindustrial, or other slack spaces left for nonlandowners to appropriate? Art Camp emerged somewhere between these two positions, conceived as speculative research for children and artists. The idea was to explore the potential of derelict or underdetermined predevelopment plots as sites to establish the habit of appropriating limited resources for creative uses and so grow policy through experience. After Art Camp and the associated research project, we coauthored design guidance that did begin to safeguard space for making.

Often, we go to situations, and we see the intrinsic value in things. It is a strategy that is not always visible to the naked eye.

Liza   Altab Ali Park in Whitechapel is such a project. A small area of green in East London named after a murdered garment worker. The space is a former church yard, and, in the corner, there is the Shaheed Minar monument, commemorating those killed in the 1952 Bengali language demonstrations in Dhaka. The design drew on research of the histories of use of the space beyond the built fabric. We made the process of unearthing histories performative and shared. The built can be reappropriated in unimagined ways. The site was extremely layered, there had been four churches on it. Our investigations included public archaeological digs with 750 people participating. The final project includes the marking of the profile of one of the church's fragments and imagined fragments of another alongside giving a new setting to the monuments.

Francesca You have laid the groundwork from the very beginning as sort of subversive, with your name alone, and disruptive with developers. Are there advantages to being difficult?

Katherine It has been about recognizing anger. Not just our anger but the anger of others as well. It has been about being able to legitimize anger as a response to the status quo and having that acknowledged. We try not to spend time convincing the doubters; rather, we seek out and build coalitions with those who are not even yet part of the process. And we recognize the inequality of need and amplify that against the often simplistic decision-making process via the majority.

Francesca What has your transdisciplinary partnership, which is founded on artistic practice, meant for your work in the built environment and the public realm?

Katherine What I always found fascinating about working with architects is that they have this tremendous responsibility to know everything about a situation. They are culturally positioned to have a solution before they start. Our practice works from a position of complete speculation. Not being tasked to know everything and, in fact, finding out what you do not know drives the practice. It is an investigation of doubt or ambiguity.

Liza   It has allowed us to work in an expanded field of architecture. A confidence to create spaces that are open-ended is both meaning and use. Our design of the Wonderlab gallery at the Science Museum in London, for example: Is it a place where an exhausted parent can recover or is it a place for children to learn about science? It is really both. All projects hold questions, and we do not necessarily share them with those who commission us.

Francesca How important is the emotional and the empathetic in your work, the qualities that are often described as feminine qualities? Is this something that is breaking the framework of architectural practice? Bringing the emotive into the design agenda and process?

Liza   It is the imaging of what is needed—whether the bench designed to lean back and take up space in the street or edging a public stage with a backdrop of a cherry blossom for celebratory public moments. At times we have talked about ourselves as double agents. We get the commercial brief, and we insert the unpaid-for pleasure into it. But we are triple agents in the end, because we are bringing two forms of value into one. Because a successful, well-loved site tends to add all sorts of value, including the monetary.

Francesca What is your message to the next generation of women in the field?

Liza   I think some of them are more effective than us and seem better at being charming and even-tempered. Honestly, I could say: What can we learn from *them*? We want to go on practicing, so we are learning from *you*!

Katherine Clarke & Liza Fior

Barking Town Square

Year 2011
Client Redrow Regeneration with the London Borough of Barking and Dagenham

The scheme resolutely carves out a shared civic space from a commercially driven development for Barking, in the far East of London. It has four interlocking elements: a civic square, an arboretum, a folly wall, and an arcade. The civic square is an extra large outdoor room, faced by the elevations of the town hall, the library, and the folly wall. It serves as a flexible space for events and is furnished with pale pink stretch benches on a floor of pink Spanish granite. It is linked to the arboretum via a stage of reclaimed timber. The folly recovers the texture of Barking's lost historic fabric and stands as a *memento mori* to this current cycle of regeneration built from salvaged fragments. An arboretum of forty mature trees of sixteen different species, arranged to create settings of varied scales and character, bring a forest to the center of the town and add reverie and escape to the lexicon of ambitions for public space. These spaces are connected by a catwalk of black-and-white tiles under overscaled lamps.

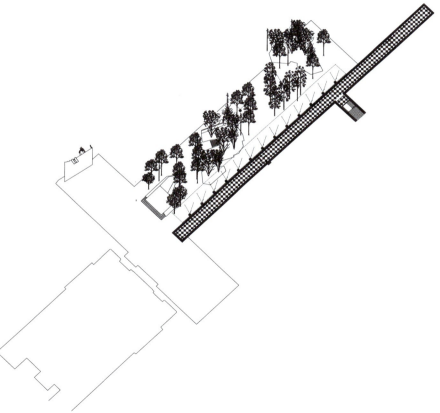

Altab Ali Park

Year 2012
Client London Borough of Tower Hamlets and the Greater London Authority

Altab Ali Park is one of three open spaces by muf that make a connection between the City of London and the Olympic Park. Named after a murdered garment worker, and the site of three successive churches, it is now the site of the Shaheed Minar monument. The renovation of the park is a transformation of a valued but dilapidated open space in an area heavy with traffic and with few green spaces. This park is understood as a microcosm of the local area, where, historically, many different cultural, religious, and political influences have shaped the fabric and lives of the people who lived there. The new garden acknowledges the secular and sacred multilayered history and character of the Whitechapel neighborhood, after a public historical dig involving 750 people marking those lost churches and creating a setting for the Shaheed Minar. Although small in area, muf honored this complex history with commissions such as hand-carved stone fragments. It is now a successful shared space for adults and children to appropriate for play, rest, and to mark important occasions, from International Language Day to public protests.

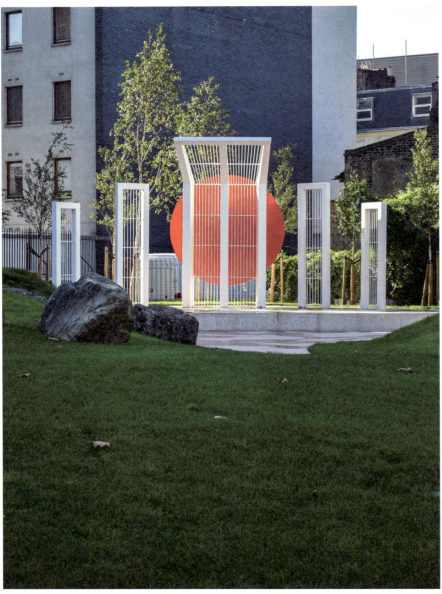

**TREADING
LIGHTLY
ALTAB ALI**

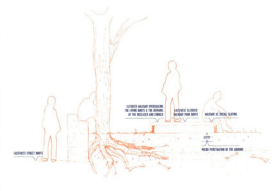

King's Crescent

Year   2018
Client   **London Borough of Hackney**

To play in a street is to play with the expectations of use of a street. King's Crescent is a housing estate in East London where new mixed-tenure housing was added and the existing buildings refurbished. Muf worked from first principles with the wider team of architects. Placing a shared public realm at the center of the scheme, a new playable street now runs through the center of the estate. Both route and destination, the street creates a new connection to nearby Clissold Park and is a shared space for residents and neighbors from the immediate and wider area. From a formal point of view, it reflects the flow of children's play and their continuous exploration and understanding of observed and lived experience. Play is given its territory as part of the everyday essentials of the city, a shared space for adults and children. It is shared ground, tenure blind; it belongs to those who live on it, but it is also a shortcut to the park. Like all public spaces, playable spaces require the "furniture" to make it your own for the time you spend there, from bespoke props for play to social furniture.

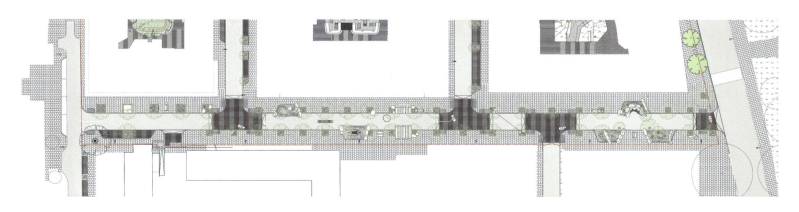

Ruskin Square

Year 2010–ongoing, phased delivery
Client Stanhope PLC

In this project, the extensive mixed-use site is privately owned, but all outdoor space is publicly accessible. Muf brought to the project a body of research not only on making public spaces but on making space public. The studio has led on the design of all open spaces and public realm over a twelve-year period, from meanwhile uses to inform the initial designs to bespoke street furniture to ensure that all spaces invite the neighborhood in to make it their own. Muf has played back the *site branding* in their designs, drawing on John Ruskin's concerns with the natural world, the arts, and his belief in the value of play, thereby creating in the design settings for everyday life beyond consumption, for all ages. Natural stone "mountains" for adventurous play and outside rooms edged with characterful trees create spaces for play, gatherings, and respite. The design is underpinned by ambitious water management, a permeable landscape where the needs of natural and social ecologies are prioritized.

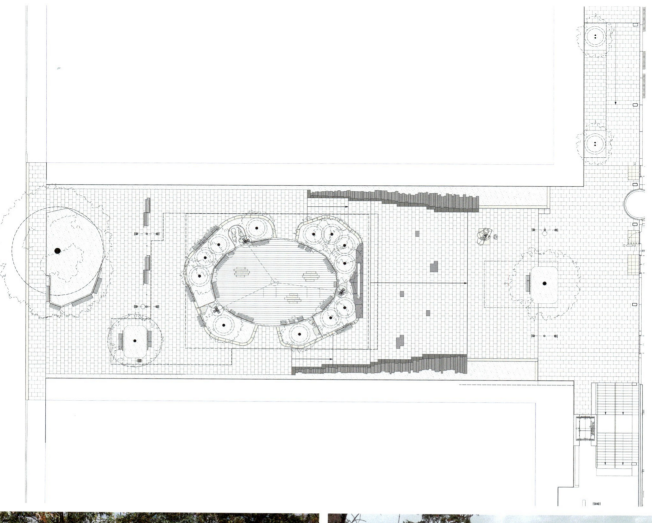

Wonderlab

Year   2017
Client   **Science Museum, London**

Can the museum offer a blueprint for public space? The Wonderlab gallery at London's Science Museum communicates scientific principles through spaces of spectacle and retreat. The 2,500-square-meter gallery and attendant spaces are designed to allow the visitor to move around, led by curiosity, while the adjacencies of spaces open up inherent relationships between light and sound. Formally, echoes of well-known spaces of scientific discovery and learning can be found in the design: Faraday's lecture hall can be seen in the show space, the orrery recalls Joseph Wright of Derby's famous painting, and a visit to the historic but still-in-use chemistry labs in Oxford inspired the Chemistry Bar. Muf has created a robust, hardworking space which also delivers a sense of grandeur, mystery, and delight. It is visited by hundreds of thousands of people each year, including children from UK schools who can visit for free. Muf designed the gallery and much of its contents in collaboration with experts, from scientists to artists, engineers to craftspeople.

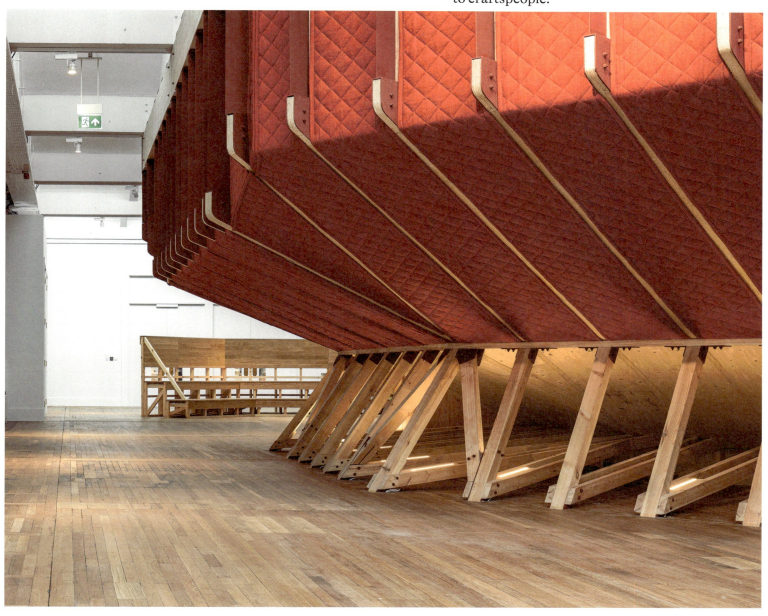

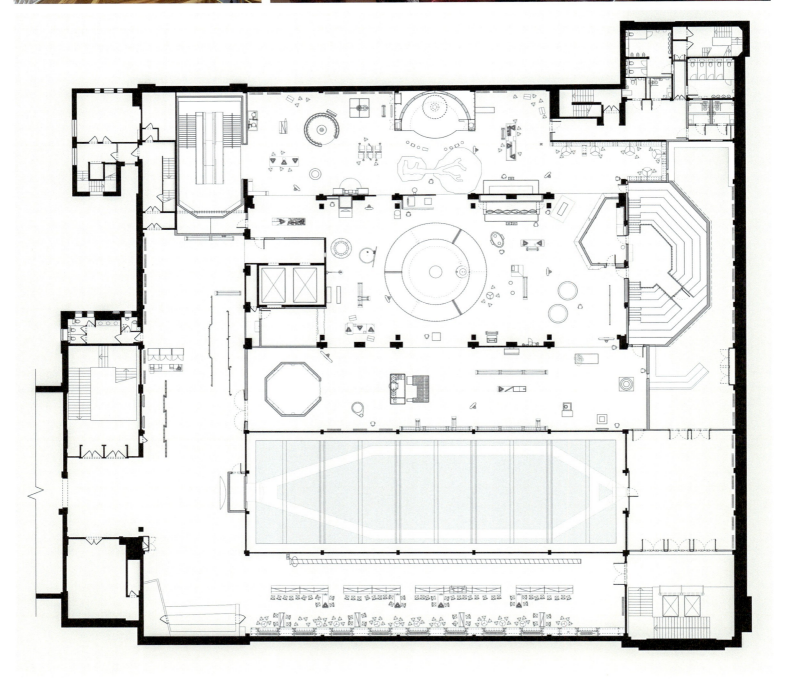

Noella Nibakuze

The Rwandan architect Noella Nibakuze strives to establish an authentically Rwandan architectural narrative. With no architectural programs in Rwanda at the time, she moved to South Africa in 2005 to study architectural technology. In 2012, with two degrees and acquired new skills, she moved back to her home country and became one of the first fifty nationally certified architects in Rwanda. Today, Noella Nibakuze works as a design director at the Kigali office of MASS Design Group. There, she is equally a contributor to a women's platform that lends services to women-led communities and serves as a mentor to architecture students and young professionals in the field. With her work, Noella Nibakuze aims to promote the use of local materials and labor, focusing on architectural design, construction administration, building technology, and sustainability. She is also passionate about encouraging young and ambitious women to pursue careers in STEM and design. In 2020, she was an architectural design mentor on sustainable architecture to ten young Rwandan women artists participating in the Green Architecture Project, a six-month project initiated by the Soul of Nations Foundation.

Born in 1985 in Rwanda
Since 2017 design director at Mass Design Group, Kigali Studio. MASS (Model of Architecture Serving Society) Design Group was founded in 2008 as an NPO with the mission to research, design, build, and advocate for architecture that promotes justice and human dignity.
Based in Kigali, Rwanda
www.massdesigngroup.org

"Lack of inclusion, whether it is because of race, gender, or cultural or educational background is an obstacle to innovation."

Noella Nibakuze is one of the leading young architects at MASS Design Group in Kigali, Rwanda. She is deeply committed to rebuilding her country, its culture, and to furthering African architecture while making this a sustainable journey that is part of a much bigger agenda within communities and for local economies. Francesca Ferguson met her via Zoom across continents to talk about what has driven her resolute agenda.

Francesca What does diversity in architecture mean to you? How have you experienced the issues that surround it on your career path?

Noella To me, diversity in architecture is about bringing voices from different backgrounds, cultures, and perspectives to design and the built environment. Lack of inclusion, whether it is because of race, gender, or cultural or educational background, is an obstacle to innovation. When I started studying architecture in South Africa, in my first-year class of about a hundred people, only eight of us were black and only two were black women. This is when it hit me: I am one of very few. During internships, I was acutely aware of the lack of representation in office leadership. It was usually a white man or a black man leading the company. In such environments, it can be intimidating to bring your ideas fully to the table. It can make people feel that they need to work twice as hard to be heard. For me, it made it difficult to see what my future in the architecture industry would look like. With my experience now, I can confidently say that we need greater input and ideas from a wider range of perspectives.

Francesca Do you find it, paradoxically, empowering to have this mission and to be in such a minority as a woman in the field?

Noella Not in the long run. It might feel good, especially for a young person's ego, but as I have progressed into this male-dominated profession, I have come to realize that I need my peers with me.

Francesca You grew up in a country that had just come out of the 1994 genocide against the Tutsi and did not have a school of architecture at the time. What steps did you take to enter the profession? How did the cultural and political climate of your training years define your position and practice?

Noella After the 1994 genocide against the Tutsi, there was a collective desire to rebuild, particularly within my generation, and this influenced my perseverance in architecture school. I wanted to rebuild my country along with other Rwandans. Since there were no schools of architecture in Rwanda at the time (the first one opened in 2008), I went to study abroad. By the time I had completed my undergraduate studies, I was fortunate to continue my education through a government-funded scholarship for women in STEM. And so, my journey has been a mix of venturing forward on my own but also receiving support from the government. This has given me an appreciation for how necessary it is, in my current practice, to illuminate the path forward for the new generation of Rwandan architects.

Francesca Once you qualified, you were not drawn to the high-end architecture practices in South Africa and the kind of global building design. Why not?

Noella I noticed that when I was studying the history of architecture, we were predominantly learning about Western architecture but very little about African architecture. So, I came to appreciate local architecture that was public and accessible while studying and moving through South African architecture. I became much more attracted to the kind of work that would serve more people and bring me closer to those who could not afford to hire an architect on their own.

Francesca In 2017, you joined MASS Design Group, their practice in Kigali. What is it about MASS that was decisive to you as you compare the work environments that you have been in?

Noella I was drawn to contribute to an architecture that was rooted in people, place, materials, and culture, and MASS was already doing the kind of work that I aspired to. I have been able to work on projects that are very hands-on, where we use local materials and immerse ourselves within the communities that we serve. Doing this work within a diverse collective was another draw: MASS is a collective of over 250 architects, engineers, landscape architects, storytellers, product designers, and more, representing about twenty nationalities, with more than half of the Kigali-based studio being women.

Francesca What is needed to create a good foundation for women in the profession, and how are you engaged in that?

Noella Throughout my time in school and at work, I have seen women drop out of the profession because they do not have the support to successfully blend their personal and work lives. If we want more women in the field of architecture, we need to create an environment that allows women to lead meaningful personal lives and pursue career growth. For example, providing flexible working hours for mothers, availing childcare support at the office, and, more importantly, putting in place company policies that support women. At MASS, we have a women's group where we support each other, share challenges and resources, recruit and train young professionals in the field, and lend our expertise to other women-led organizations. Another challenge that young women in the architecture school face is the lack of role models and people they can see themselves in. Personally, I have found it important and rewarding to teach at the School of Architecture and Built Environment at the University of Rwanda. My hope is that young women in universities can see themselves represented and be inspired by their lecturers and start to envision their own journey early on.

Francesca You are a crusader for change on so many levels. Tell me about RICA (the Rwanda Institute for Conservation Agriculture), the community-based practice and the learned experience that can enlighten us on the path to sustainability.

Noella   RICA is an agricultural campus that MASS designed and engineered. It is made up of sixty-nine buildings, designed specifically for the courses that would be taught there. The project started in 2017 and is nearing completion [completed as of February 2023]. From the start, we immersed ourselves in the community. We approached the local government, farmers, builders, artisans, and residents and engaged them as an integral part of the building process. This proximity gave us knowledge we might not have come across as readily — which local materials were available, who to partner with, and so on. It was also an opportunity to share the objectives of the project and extend a sense of ownership to the local community. Ninety-five percent of RICA's workforce was hired locally, and ninety-six percent by weight, of the building's materials were sourced locally. In addition, we trained a good number of the local community, equipping them with skills beyond this project.

Francesca There are many ramifications beyond the act of construction and building.

Noella   Exactly. We believe the benefactors of the building should not only be the client but the community at large.

Francesca In terms of local materials, local resources, and sustainable building, what do you think architects in the Western, Eurocentric sphere could learn from the RICA campus as a project and in its materiality?

Noella   Our goal with RICA was to prototype and test local, low-embodied carbon materials. We used rammed earth walls, timber instead of steel roof structures, and stone instead of concrete for the foundations. With ninety-six percent of the materials being sourced locally, it was relatively easy to track and measure the embodied carbon of the materials we were using, hence the embodied carbon of the buildings at RICA are about two-thirds of the global average for institutional projects. While these materials might not be available or the best choice everywhere, applying the same principle of sourcing materials as locally as possible is recommended. Partnering with local manufacturers, artisans, co-ops, and entrepreneurs often meant that businesses were scaling up quickly to meet our demand. We provided training to some partners and, overall, the project was an opportunity to expand the capacities of the local community and a learning experience for us.

Francesca It is a huge spectrum in terms of sustainability and holistic approach. It shows the economic ramifications, too, because it is boosting local enterprise and local trade.

Noella   Yes, understanding local supply chains helped us to find and develop the right partners. We were able to source most of the materials locally, which boosted the local economy. The project also created jobs for the community, whereby over 1,700 construction workers were employed, and more than eighty-five local artisans and entrepreneurs were involved in bringing RICA to life.

Francesca As one of the first finalists, how do you think the issue of diversity of this award can be further developed?

Noella   The award is an opportunity to showcase and elevate the work of women in the field. My hope is that the award will grow to celebrate a wide range of women doing different kinds of work within architecture who might not be profiled enough to be nominated for this award. I was the only East African nominee this year but, of course, there are many other women in the region doing great work!

Francesca What is your advice to young women in the profession of architecture?

Noella   Know that you are capable and, where possible, find a mentor! This does not have to be someone you meet every day. It could be anyone in the profession that you want to join. Learn about their journey as you create your own. After all, there are many professions in the field of architecture: you could be a designer, a writer, a photographer, a curator, or an academic. The possibilities are endless.

Rwanda Institute for Conservation Agriculture

Year   2017–23
Client   Howard G. Buffett Foundation

As design director at MASS Design Group, Noella Nibakuze led the construction of the Rwanda Institute for Conservation Agriculture (RICA) project, a 1,400-hectare agricultural campus. Designed with the "One Health" approach that considers how the health of people, animals, and the environment are intertwined, it is meant to train Rwanda's next generation of leaders in agriculture while supporting national priorities for agricultural development. Located in Gashora, Eastern Province in Rwanda, it has sixty-nine buildings, all with unique and specific agricultural/campus programs. The community was an integral part of the building process, which resulted in ninety-five percent of the labor force being hired locally. RICA utilizes ninety-six percent of materials (by weight) from Rwanda, a 1.5-megawatt solar farm produces one hundred percent of RICA's electricity, and the campus sources and treats all water on-site. MASS designed, engineered, and tested local, low-embodied carbon materials, including timber roof structures, rammed earth, and compressed stabilized earth blocks.

Water Re-Use
· Stormwater Stitches
· Water Collection
· Water Filtration
· Reduce Erosion
· Reduce Siltation

Recreation & Social Areas
· Sports Courts
· Hammock Grove
· Shared Ammenities
· Study Space
· Passive & Active
· Varied Scales

Smallholder Experience
· Orchard Varietals (resilience)
· Typical Livestock
· Agroforestry Techniques
· Soil Building

Papyrus Ecosystem
· Clean Water
· Preserve Trees
· Crowned Crane Habitat
· Save Existing Trees

Forest Preserve

Faculty Housing

Spine

First Year Farms

Buffer

Wetland

Lake

Ecology Stitch
· Pollinator Gardens
· Wind Barrier
· Groundwater Recharge
· Native Habitat Corridor
· Stormwater Filtration

Conservation
· Saved Significant Trees
· Biophillia
· Carbon Sequestration
· Medicinal Plantings
· Habitat
· Seed Bank of Natives

Soil Health
· Reuse of Livestock Manure
· No Till Agriculture
· Maintain Termite Mounds
· Wind Rows To Reduce Erosion
· Reuse of Green Fertilizer

Agricultural Research
· Faculty Research Plots
· Student Research Plots
· Crop Resiliency Study
· Climate Adaptive Species

Propagation & Seed Bank
· Seed Bank for Rare Species
· Returning Species
· On-site propagation of natives
· On-site Nursery/Screenhouses

Mugusera Wetlands
· Drought storage
· Flood control
· Source of the Nile
· At risk of invasives
· At risk of sedimentation

Pasture

Enterprise: Dairy

Spine

Enterprise: Vegetable & Fruit Crops

Buffer

Wetland

Lake

Environmental Siting
· Minimize solar gain
· Maximize ventilation
· Nature daylighting
· Preserve trees for cooling

Energy & Water Infrastructure
· Water treatment plant
· Lowered carbon footprint
· Visible methods
· Integrates native vegetation & habitat
· Open system reduces maintenance

KEY
1 ENTRY
2 SOCIAL SPACE
3 BEDROOM
4 LOUNGE
5 KITCHENETTE
6 BATHROOMS
7 STUDENT LIFE

Masaka Affordable Housing

Year   **2017–19**
Client   **Remote Group**

Encompassing 26,750 square meters, Masaka Affordable Housing provides an eco-urbanist model for neighborhood design solutions to the housing needs of Rwanda's expanding urban population. Counteracting trends of overcrowding, informality, and sprawl, Masaka responds to the spatial needs of Rwandan urban dwellers across 281 living units by increasing density in a culturally responsive and climate-adapted manner, using low-cost and locally fabricated building technologies. The development integrates green spaces and infrastructure across five hectares, providing public pedestrian corridors, public transit extensions, and permeable paving to improve climate resilience. A mix of housing typologies ensure that dwellings are both affordable and culturally sensitive. The project pioneers the use of aerated autoclaved concrete construction as a cost-effective, made-in-Rwanda building technology. As part of the design team, Noella Nibakuze aimed to understand the cultural context and the needs of the future urban dwellers. She researched the vernacular architecture of Rwanda and conducted interviews with the local community and potential new homebuyers.

S		Shop or studio for a single professional or a young couple
M		Apartment for a young couple with children
M		Townhouse for a government-/ business-sector employee
M		Townhouse for a middle-class family
L		Townhouse for a middle-class family, both parents working
L		Semidetached house for a middle-class family, three members working

Infectious Disease Re-search Institute

Year   2019–ongoing
Client   Lagos State Ministry of Health

As testing laboratories remain limited across the continent, Africa continues to be susceptible to novel infectious diseases. To prevent the next pandemic outburst, the Lagos State Ministry of Health is developing their Mainland Hospital Campus into a hub for cutting-edge infectious disease treatment and research. MASS first partnered with the Lagos State Ministry of Health in 2019 to develop prototypical health facilities and has continued this partnership toward the design of the Lagos Infectious Disease Research Institute (LIDRI), led by Noella Nibakuze. Working in a new geographic location with a different climate from Rwanda allowed for an opportunity for research and to adapt the strategies and principles. While Rwanda has a moderate climate and calls for passive design strategies and principles such as natural daylight and natural cooling and heating, Lagos is hot and humid. Therefore, it demands careful environmental design that uses both passive and hybrid comfort strategies and principles and the installation of efficient building services systems.

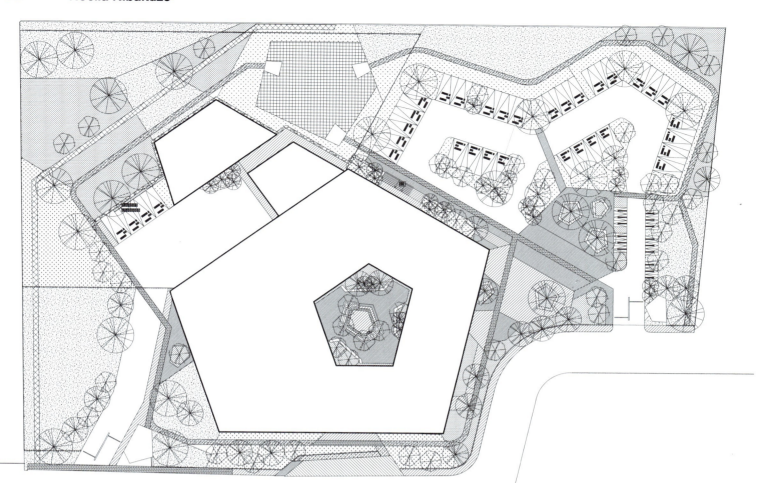

Tosin Oshinowo

Architect, entrepreneur, author, and public speaker: Nigerian visionary Tosin Oshinowo is a woman of many creative talents. Educated in the United Kingdom and with work experience in various architectural firms across Europe and Africa, she returned to Lagos in 2009. Inspired by the city's creative freedom, flexibility, and brimming potential, she played a key role in developing the Nigerian capital into the epicenter of architecture and design that it is today.

In 2012, Tosin Oshinowo established cmDesign Atelier, an architectural studio where she functions as the founding principal and leads a team of seven architects and project managers. Their style is modernist, clean, and sets out to incorporate as much light as possible. Renowned for her expansive residential and commercial spaces, Tosin Oshinowo is familiar with high-profile, luxurious projects. But her work follows a deeper vision. It centers around Afro-minimalism, striving to include a "truly African aesthetic" without external influences. It is about translating cultural authenticity into physical buildings, reflecting how African communities interact and use spaces.

In addition to her architectural endeavors, Tosin Oshinowo also runs her own brand, Ilé Ilà, which designs contemporary furniture using local African fabrics. Her interests also go into the conceptual sphere, with the aim to support African design and innovation.

Born in 1980 in Nigeria
Established her studio cmDesign Atelier in 2012
Based in Lagos, Nigeria
www.cmdesign-atelier.com

"Great creativity comes out of great struggle. Lagos is very much the epitome of that."

Tosin Oshinowo is an architect, educator, and curator based in Lagos, Nigeria, who leads the architectural practice cmDesign Atelier and the lifestyle furniture company Ilé Ilà. She is a registered architect in the Federal Republic of Nigeria and a member of the Royal Institute of British Architects. Among her recent projects are Ngarannam Village, a United Nations Development Program (UNDP) resettlement project for the village that had come under attack in 2014 by the militant Islamist group Boko Haram. Other significant works include Maryland Mall, several private residences in Lagos and the surrounding areas, and numerous arts and product design collaborations. Stella Lee sat with her for an online interview, during which they discussed Tosin's beginnings in the profession. Further along in their conversation, they got into the disconnect between academia and practice, the pitfalls of a colonialist mentality in design, and the importance of nurturing a deeper understanding of the cultures of the end-user clients. They also touched upon Tosin's curatorial work for the upcoming Sharjah Architecture Triennial in November 2023, in which scarcity and beauty are thematically aligned.

Stella   How did you find your way into architecture?

Tosin   I knew at about the age of twelve that this is what I wanted to do. I had excelled at visual arts in school. My father was having a home built, his intended retirement home, and showed me the floor plans. I was so excited! I was able to fully understand them and took a big interest in following him to the building when it was being constructed. Funnily enough, I am now doing the renovation of the house because he wants to extend the ground floor as he is getting older and does not want to climb stairs. It is funny how things have come full circle. This really was my first understanding of the idea that you have to curate an interesting experience in space. However, I did not acquire any decent skills in this until I got to university to study architecture.

Stella   You studied abroad, in London. Was this your first time leaving Lagos?

Tosin   Yes, I left Nigeria at sixteen after doing my A levels and went to university in the United Kingdom. However, after finishing my first degree, I was really struggling to understand the cultural nuances of why the architecture of where I was from was not the same as the architecture of where I was going to school. At the end of the first degree, I was not sure I wanted to be an architect anymore and de-

cided to change schools. I found a course at UCL [University College London] called Urban Design and Development, which specifically looked at urban design in developing cities, and I just thought: "This is it, this is what I am missing!" I did not know enough about where I was from, and this is the reason why I did not feel rooted in what I was doing. This course is what changed it for me. I learned about where I was from through books. I read and read, and there was one particular module in which you had to write six essays that spoke about your city's origins and the political, cultural, and economic circumstances that explain why it is where it is. This process helped ground my understanding of where I came from. I used the additional confidence and clarity this gave me to go back and do my part two at the Architectural Association.

Stella   It is interesting that it took moving away from home to learn more about where you came from. How was it to return to Lagos after spending time abroad with your studies and work experiences?

Tosin   I had to learn how to do business in this environment that I had left as a teenager. I did not have a network. I met people by working in a local practice, which helped me find my footing. Academia will teach you to be a good designer, but it does not teach you anything about business at all. Architects need to understand where clients are coming from. If there is a way that you can value-engineer your project to get it to the costs that the client can afford without compromising too much, this is where you need to be. It is not enough to sit in your position and say: "No, I want it like this." You are not paying for it. When architects start to really understand the value of money and give the client the intangible of helping to ensure that their assets stay profitable, then you are in a much better position.

Stella   Could you speak a bit about the Ngarannam Village project in Borno? I was struck in particular by an interview you gave in which you explained the choice to install latrines instead of toilet bowls.

Tosin   When we started the project, I went to speak to the committee. And remember, there are many stakeholders and government officials. But ultimately, there was an end-user. If someone is not used to using a toilet, they will stand on the seats. It also goes back to the fundamentals of our profession. We need to understand who our end-user is and design accordingly. If you go where the people live, and you see how they cook, you realize that they do not need an indoor kitchen because they cook on a wood stove. There is a very big difference between being progressive and understanding people and creating what they need. They need a safe environment so they can thrive and rebuild their lives. What they need is a place they can call home that takes into consideration their cultural nuances. Sadly, this is one of the challenges we have had with colonialism. Somebody came and said: "Oh, this is barbaric, let's change it." As I become more enlightened about my culture and what would have probably been the religion of the day, I am very aware that we have lost so much to an idea of progress. A lot of where I am finding myself as a designer is looking for cultural nuances that I can reimpose into my buildings by working with materials in an experimental way. A good example of this is what we have done in Ngarannam with the Tyrolean, the red soil that was used to finish the walls. Hopefully, this contributes to a knowledge base that will continue to evolve in a direction that creates an awareness of our identity through physical forms.

Stella   Diversity means different things in different contexts. What does diversity mean in Nigeria?

Tosin   We are a country where somebody just drew a line and said: "Go for it, be a country." We have so many different ethnic groups. There are a lot of internal tensions, and I think this has been one of the biggest challenges we have politically. It is very much a patriarchal society as well. It has become less and less the case for me over time, as the better you are known in your industry, the work takes precedence. But every time you meet new clients, a set of consultants, or are working with someone who might not know you personally, you do have a little bit of a struggle and have to constantly prove yourself. You have to carry yourself with firmness and let them know that you are the architect and that you are the person that they need to listen to. If you go too far in the other direction, they just see you as a mean woman. So, it is a difficult balance.

Stella   Could you speak a bit about the Sharjah Architecture Triennial coming up in November this year?

Tosin   Yes, I am curating the triennial, and it is called *The Beauty of Impermanence: An Architecture of Adaptability.* And to be honest, this is my coming-out party because this is where I fully celebrate everything that has made me a designer today. What is important for me to celebrate is the acknowledgment that there are so many people who work from conditions of scarcity, who are constantly innovating and adapting to the constraints within which they work. The irony is that, as we live within our current climatic challenges, many more Global North countries and cities are now dealing with these same challenges of scarcity.

The lessons we can learn from the continent about how we have adapted could be a starting point for a mobile solution that is not always about resource extraction or consumption. Great creativity comes out of great struggle. Lagos is very much the epitome of that, and there are so many designers that we are beginning to see as a result of this kind of bubbling above the surface. But it has been fermenting for a very long time over the last twenty years. We are really beginning to have a diversity of voices and an interest from people who are genuinely looking for another way of approaching some of the challenges that we face.

Ngarannam Village

Year   2020–22
Client   UNDP Nigeria

Tosin Oshinowo was leading the design vision for the UNDP project to rebuild Ngarannam, a village in rural northeastern Nigeria. It had become deserted between 2013 and 2015, following various attacks by the Islamist militant group Boko Haram. Countless families were forced out of their homes, mainly taking refuge in Maiduguri and in Mafa, and thousands of people are still living in camps today. Their shelter, access to basic services, and local leadership structures were fragmented. The process of rebuilding Ngarannam includes the construction of more than 500 housing units for over 2,500 residents, a health clinic, a primary school, a marketplace, a community center, and other services including road infrastructure. For the housing units, Tosin Oshinowo developed further the resettlement design executed by UNDP and improved its look and feel while taking into consideration the sustainability of the building structure. Working with the community, she paid regular site visits to ensure a "human-centered design" that is suited to their needs and customs. The logistics and access to the construction site were proven to be challenging and required a military resort. In addition, there was limited time available during visits to inspect the works, which required heavy reliance on technology communication through the construction process with the team on the ground.

Rensource Energy Office

Year   **2018–19**
Client   **Rensource Energy Nigeria**

Located on Victoria Island in Lagos, Rensource Energy Nigeria is a leading renewable energy company operating across Nigeria. The brief was to design a defunct Oceanic Bank Building to accommodate the company with a young team, driven by the mission to encourage positive change in a country known for its oil production. The space reflects the company's values, identity, and mission. As such, the exterior of the building was designed using solar panels as a key aesthetic element. This project was the retrofit of a nineteen-seventies building that had undergone an extension in the mid-nineties. CmDesign Atelier addressed several structural challenges to ensure the viability of the retrofit within the existing envelope. The building services also had to be upgraded to accommodate the new occupancy in addition to their design intent of creating a light and refreshing environment, all within a conservative budget.

The Lantern House

Year   2020–22
Client   Private

The Lantern house was designed for a Lagosian family on the private Banana Island. The 911-square-meter, five-bedroom house is sustainability-conscious and entirely powered by solar energy. It represents Tosin Oshinowo's signature style, with clean and crisp lines, as well as sophisticated geometric patterning to emphasize depth, texture, and materiality. One of the essential features is the double helical staircase which runs through the building. The house had to be accommodated on a land allocation—two-thirds of the standard size. This brought challenges during construction and required a methodology that ensured the intent could be achieved with as little compromise to the expected finish as possible. For example, the helical stairs were cast at the end of the project, while temporary stairs were used to move materials and finishes through the building.

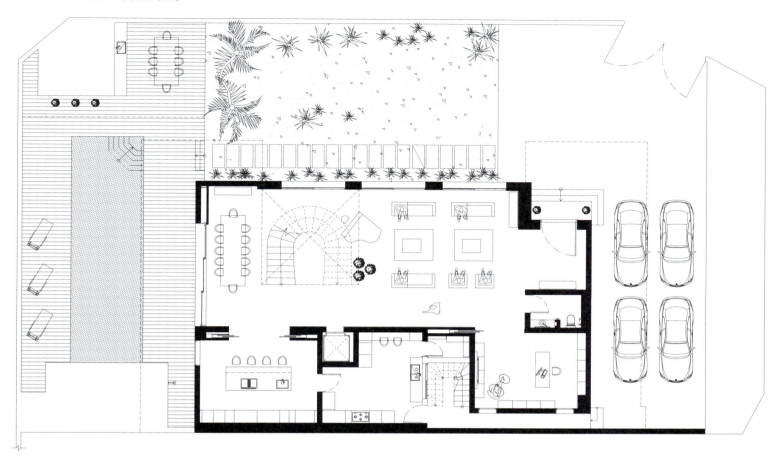

Ground floor

First floor   Second floor

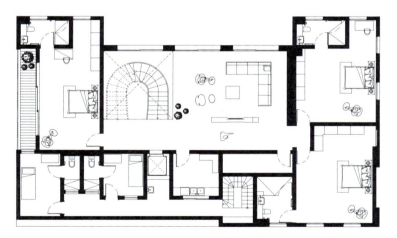

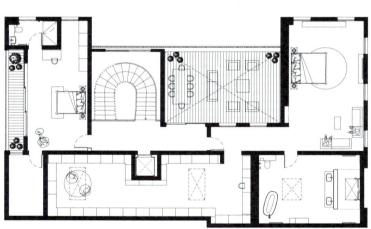

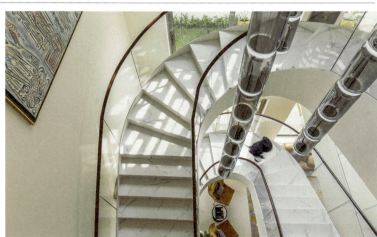

Coral Pavilion

Year 2019–22
Client private

Located on Ilashe Beach in Lagos, this minimalist beach pavilion with low, clean lines was created for a young family from Lagos. The building is open to the elements and is designed to take full advantage of the consistent breeze yet is protected from the sun and rain by its roof and overhang. Cultural elements, such as the bar patterns inspired by those used by Nigeria's Kanuri people, were also added to the design. The simplicity of this project screens its structural complexity. There are four 4.1-meter cantilever beams with three 13-meter transfer beams. The base also incorporated a cantilever slab edge to give the illusion of floating above the sand. These were all achieved using bamboo scaffolding, working closely with the structural engineer and the contractor to ensure the simplicity of the form was completed.

Sencillo Beach House

Year 2017–18
Client Private

With the sole access to the region via water travel, the beaches along the western peninsula have remained exclusive with limited urban development. For the Sencillo beach house, located on the private Ilashe Island, Tosin Oshinowo designed a series of rose-gold, powder-coated four-millimeter-thick steel screens based on indigenous Yoruba Adire fabric patterns that protect against the sun and act as privacy screens. The idea was to create a series of spaces by using locally sourced building materials, mainly cedar wood for the tongue-and-groove doors and rotating shutter panels for the hot tub area. White concrete was used for the pool deck to avoid the monotony of a tiled surface, and polished concrete was used for all internal spaces. The frameless glass was used for the balustrade behind the laser-cut steel screens. This project was the first where cmDesign Atelier experimented with an epoxy floor finish, requiring several trials before the intended result. A significant challenge was working out the right logistics to move materials to the remote area.

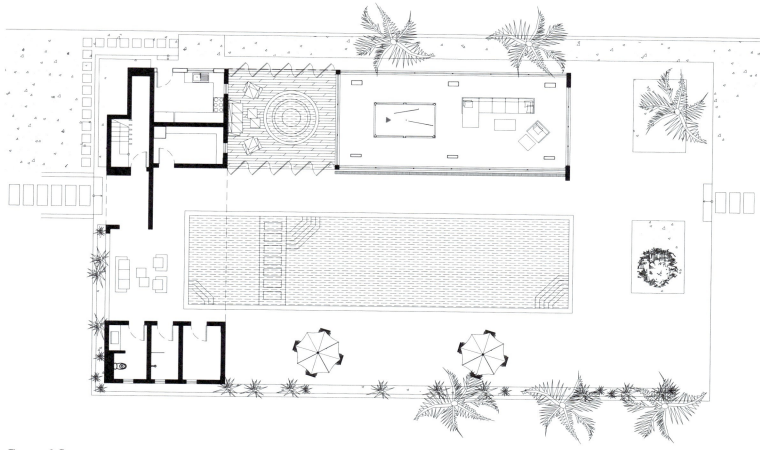

Ground floor

Diversity in Architecture e. V. was cofounded in Berlin in June 2021 by Ursula Schwitalla, Christiane Fath, Dirk Boll, Sol Camacho, Odile Decq, Angelika Fitz, Anna Heringer, and Marc Kimmich.

Chairs

Ursula Schwitalla, BDA, Honorary Senator Tuebingen University is the cofounder and chair of DIVIA. With degrees in history, geography, politics, and a PhD in art history, she works as an exhibition curator and art consultant in Tuebingen. She is also a lecturer at the Humboldt University of Berlin and the University of Tuebingen, and at the latter she has been curating the lecture series "Architecture Today" for twenty years. In 2021, she published *Women in Architecture* with Hatje Cantz.

Christiane Fath, BDA is the cofounder and deputy chair of DIVIA. She is a qualified architect, multiplier, and culture manager who offers a Berlin-based interdisciplinary platform for architecture communication. A strategic developer and curator of event formats, she is also the founder of the gallery "framework" in Berlin and Vienna. In 2021, she cocurated *Architektinnen BDA*, whose accompanying catalogue was published by Jovis. Currently, she is a visiting professor of interdisciplinary gender studies at University of Kaiserslautern-Landau.

Copy and managing editor, interviewer

Veronika Lukashevich is a journalist, editor, and author, with a master's degree in journalism from City, University of London. Based in Berlin, she also works as a freelance multilingual ghost writer of memoirs and biographies. With a focus on profile writing and long-form reporting, she delves deeply into the topics of migration, identity, and multiculturalism. She also works as an editor at DIVIA and has been editing architecture books since 2021.

Interviewers

Francesca Ferguson is a curator and founding CEO of Make_Shift agency in Berlin, working with clients within cultural heritage, urban planning, and regeneration. Her work has explored how to integrate new technologies and tools for innovation and community engagement. She is a member of DIVIA's board of trustees and is an architect with a particular interest and experience in the use of social interaction within sustainable development.

Stella Lee is an independent practitioner based in Berlin and the cofounder and former principal of Bureau V, an award-winning architecture and design practice based in New York City. She is a member of the board of trustees at DIVIA and has supported workplace equity within architecture through her writing and activism.

DIVIA's advisory board consists of architecture experts from around the globe:

Julia Albani, curator, critic, and communications strategist, based in Lisbon

Anne-Laure Cavigneaux and Rodney Eggleston, cofounders of March.Studio, based in Melbourne

Elena Fabrizi, cofounder of the creative collective RebelArchitette, based in Carrara

Julia Gamolina, editor in chief of the online platform Madame Architect, based in New York City

Martin Jasper, founding director of Jasper Architects, based between the main offices in Buenos Aires and Vienna and Berlin

Mariam Kamara, founding principal of atelier masōmī, based in Niamey and Zurich

Eduard Kögel, expert for the development of architecture and urban planning in Asia, based in Berlin

Kathrin Moore, founder of MooreUrban Design, based in San Francisco

Otobong Nkanga, Nigeria-born visual and performance artist, based in Kano and Antwerp

Francesca Perani, founder of Francesca Perani Enterprise and cofounder of RebelArchitette, based in Bergamo

Werner Sobek, founder of the sustainable design and engineering company Werner Sobek, based in Stuttgart

Brinda Somaya, architect and urban conservationist, founder of Somaya & Kalappa Consultants, based in Mumbai

Renato Turri (& Editors at World Architects), CEO and Partner at World Architects, based in Zurich.

This catalogue is published on the occasion of the first
divia award 2023, presented by Diversity in Architecture on
May 6, 2023, in Berlin

Editors
Ursula Schwitalla and Christiane Fath
Managing editor
Veronika Lukashevich
Project management
Dorothee Hahn
Copyediting
Veronika Lukashevich
Graphic design
Lamm & Kirch with Caspar Reuss,
Berlin/Leipzig
Production
Thomas Lemaître
Reproductions
Schwabenrepro GmbH, Fellbach
Printing and binding
Livonia Print, Riga
Paper
Munken Lynx, 120 g/m²

Published by
Hatje Cantz Verlag GmbH
Mommsenstraße 27
10629 Berlin
www.hatjecantz.com
A Ganske Publishing Group Company

ISBN 978-3-7757-5525-2

Printed in Latvia

Donors of Diversity in Architecture e. V.